Loving Him More
THROUGH DARKEST VALLEYS

~

SISTERS CHALLENGE CANCER
IN TWO-PART HARMONY

May you always know that you never walk alone —
Rebecca Kordatzky

REBECCA KORDATZKY

WESTBOW
PRESS®
A DIVISION OF THOMAS NELSON
& ZONDERVAN

Copyright © 2020 Rebecca Kordatzky.

All rights reserved. No part of this book may be used or reproduced by any means, graphic, electronic, or mechanical, including photocopying, recording, taping or by any information storage retrieval system without the written permission of the author except in the case of brief quotations embodied in critical articles and reviews.

This book is a work of non-fiction. Unless otherwise noted, the author and the publisher make no explicit guarantees as to the accuracy of the information contained in this book and in some cases, names of people and places have been altered to protect their privacy.

WestBow Press books may be ordered through booksellers or by contacting:

WestBow Press
A Division of Thomas Nelson & Zondervan
1663 Liberty Drive
Bloomington, IN 47403
www.westbowpress.com
1 (866) 928-1240

Because of the dynamic nature of the Internet, any web addresses or links contained in this book may have changed since publication and may no longer be valid. The views expressed in this work are solely those of the author and do not necessarily reflect the views of the publisher, and the publisher hereby disclaims any responsibility for them.

Any people depicted in stock imagery provided by Getty Images are models, and such images are being used for illustrative purposes only.
Certain stock imagery © Getty Images.

Scripture quotations marked (TLB) are taken from The Living Bible copyright © 1971. Used by permission of Tyndale House Publishers, a Division of Tyndale House Ministries, Carol Stream, Illinois 60188. All rights reserved.

Scripture quotations marked (NLT) are taken from the Holy Bible, New Living Translation, copyright ©1996, 2004, 2015 by Tyndale House Foundation. Used by permission of Tyndale House Publishers, a Division of Tyndale House Ministries, Carol Stream, Illinois 60188. All rights reserved.

Scripture quotations marked (NIV) are taken from the Holy Bible, New International Version®, NIV®. Copyright © 1973, 1978, 1984, 2011 by Biblica, Inc.™ Used by permission of Zondervan. All rights reserved worldwide. www.zondervan.com The "NIV" and "New International Version" are trademarks registered in the United States Patent and Trademark Office by Biblica, Inc.™

ISBN: 978-1-9736-9135-8 (sc)
ISBN: 978-1-9736-9134-1 (hc)
ISBN: 978-1-9736-9136-5 (e)

Library of Congress Control Number: 2020908525

Print information available on the last page.

WestBow Press rev. date: 5/29/2020

Contents

Never Ready 1
Prologue 3
Loving Him More 13
Through Darkest Valleys 59
Because I Forget So Easily 91

To my older sister, Nancy King,
who led the way for me.

With deep appreciation to Byron King and Beth Strange for their permission and encouragement to share Nancy's meditations "if her story helps even one person."

NEVER READY

The wisest has said, "There is a time for
… everything … under the sun."
Benjamin Franklin has said, "A place for everything
and everything in its place."
The mathematician proclaims the orderliness of number.
The philosopher praises clear, compelling logic.
But
when the heart has been punctured by sorrow
and is wounded by that loss,
logic and orderliness have no voice.
The sun cannot shine into that void.
We are never ready for the blackout.
Only God's love, shown through His Son, can bring warmth
and, eventually, light.

May your night be softened with the tender glow
of ministering hands,
others who know the solitude of midnight.
May the joy of dawn include healing memories
of the one who is gone but never truly departed.

NEVER READY

Prologue

The Big C

The ringing broke my dishwashing reverie. Pulled from the January snow globe picture outside my kitchen window, I hurried to the phone. Answering, I heard my doctor ask, "Are you sitting down?" My immediate reaction? I sat down, thankful that the hand-crafted telephone bench was strong and sturdy. He continued, "The biopsy shows that you have uterine cancer. We need to schedule surgery as soon as possible."

It was January 1995 when that electrifying jolt left me speechless. Quickly, surgery was scheduled for two weeks later. Thus began my personal journey with The Big C.

I was grateful that many details needed to be arranged; they gave me something productive to focus on instead of the uncertainty roused by fear of the known and the unknown. Notifying family and friends was very hard. They needed to know, but telling them was upsetting. Besides, talking about it made the situation even more real and uncertain. Fortunately, there were many other details on my list, so I chipped away—pre-op appointments to make and keep, lesson plans for the long-term substitute, parent-teacher conferences to complete, being up to date on laundry and cleaning …

On the day of surgery, I was grateful that my surgeon excelled at P&D (perseverance and details). After removing the tumor, he patiently and diligently checked the lymph nodes around the area, one by one, to see if the cancer had spread beyond the uterus. Each was cancer-free—until number seventeen, the *last* one. Examining that node, he found cancer cells waving and hollering, "Look at us! We're here!" A more accurate diagnosis: stage 4.

It was a long week in the hospital with tubes seemingly everywhere. My mind may have made up a few details, but I remember lying flat for several days and lots of ice chips. It seemed forever before I could begin taking even clear liquids. I appreciated friends who came to visit, often reporting, "You are looking great." (I'm not sure of their assessment.)

After a week in the hospital, I came home to recuperate. Immediately, friends, neighbors, and family demonstrated their support. It was amazing and affirming. The magic meal fairy was on duty for at least six weeks. I can still recite many details of who brought what. Larry and Joy brought tasty chicken wings; Wilma brought her nourishing homemade chicken noodle soup; Beverly introduced us to the best Italian dressing. And Marsha, a friend with four children and an already very full plate of responsibilities, accepted no arguments from me and came every morning for two weeks to tend to my needs and support my family. I truly felt so loved!

A month later, radiation treatments began—five days a week for three weeks. They went fairly well. More of my care army showed up; Caryn drove me every Thursday, and Kelly was my chauffeur on Tuesday. Some days I could even drive myself. At least once a week, I made sure to follow my doctors' orders to keep my nutrition up and stopped to get a chocolate shake. Now those were orders I eagerly followed.

Many others participated in my support. The staff at the cancer center provided amazing care—friendly faces, plush robes instead of hospital gowns, careful monitoring of blood stats, and more. I recall the phone support from the American Cancer Society. And the encouragement from cancer survivors was critical.

I saw the oncologist weekly. After radiation treatment number eight, I was excited to be halfway done! During the appointment that day, I experienced a stunning example of irony. My oncologist decided, "Since you are doing so well, we are going to double the number of treatments." I thought, *Um ... what a great reward?* Of course, he meant that since my body was handling the treatments with only a few side effects, we could take my plan to the next level of prevention and radiate the next level of lymph nodes. But thirty treatments instead of fifteen? Oh, my! But the day did come when I was awarded my certificate of completion.

Sisters Share Connections

The Wilson Line Up circa 1953
From left – Wanita, Mark, Lynn, Becky, Nancy, Dan

Lloyd and Ruhama Wilson and children. Circa 1958

Loving Him More through Darkest Valleys | 5

A cancer diagnosis is only one of the many connections between my sister Nancy and myself. Let me take you closer to the beginning.

I was third in the lineup of the six Wilson children. Dan was oldest and continuously forged the pathway for us. Nancy was next, a year younger than Dan. Then four years later, I was born. We three were all December babies, celebrating our birthdays within a week's time—on the tenth, twelfth, and seventeenth. As younger children, we had one birthday cake with concentric rings of candles to be blown out on successive days. I never felt cheated of singular attention around birthday time; I was proud to be included with the big kids.

Two years later, my sister Lynn joined the family. Then followed brother Mark—four and a half years younger than me. And sister Wanita was welcomed the following year.

My Personal Mother Hen

Mother Hen Nancy

Why do the lambs shake their tails?

Nancy was born to nurture, and upon my birth, she assumed the role of my personal mother hen. Besides, she loved playing with a live doll. Apparently, I didn't talk until I was three; my point and grunt sent Nancy or Dan to get what I wanted. In return, they had my undying loyalty.

Growing up on a dairy farm meant all of us shared the bonds of work, as we could—feeding calves, herding cattle to the woods for pasture, milking cows, driving tractor for the hay baler, weeding in the garden, working on Labor Day. We also shared fun—playing with kittens and puppies, riding horses, driving the pony and cart to the woods for picnics, swimming in the pond, devouring heaps of freshly harvested sweet corn. We honed our skills searching for the perfect hot spot while roasting marshmallows around many campfires. Then we often were off on a hay ride. We shared activities such as 4-H and the county fair, church youth group, and summer camp.

Nancy modeling her 4-H sewing project at the county fair

Nancy was my fountain of knowledge. We shared a bedroom and, thus, many late-night gab sessions. Some of the things she taught me might have been better left to someone else, for the outcomes were iffy at times. For example, Nancy is the one who taught me to drive our small gray Ford tractor with dual brakes and dual clutches. Struggling to understand when and how to use which pedal, my memory is indelibly imprinted with a picture of a fast-approaching ditch with Nancy in the way. Fortunately, she was a quick jumper. (Also, fortunately, she did not teach me to drive a car.)

While Hickory Point Farm was not as diverse as Noah's Ark, that didn't slow her down. There were plenty of cats, kittens, puppies, dogs, ponies, horses, cows, calves, and pigs. We also had mean roosters and aggressive goats. And Nancy cared about them all. I remember watching the horse colt that decided it was a lap dog, awkwardly trying to fold herself onto Nancy's lap multiple times. Even as a preteen, she was an active attendant at many births on the farm.

Our chosen careers were connected. Nancy worked hard to earn her nurse's cap and wore it with pride and honor for forty years. Her connection to my life's career? Of course, I couldn't be a nurse. I had to take a different route to assert my independence and therefore went into teaching. Besides, my medical expertise is made up of "Here's a Band-Aid. Take two aspirin and call the doctor in the morning." But Nancy's choice of nursing was logical. With her tender heart, she cared for all living things.

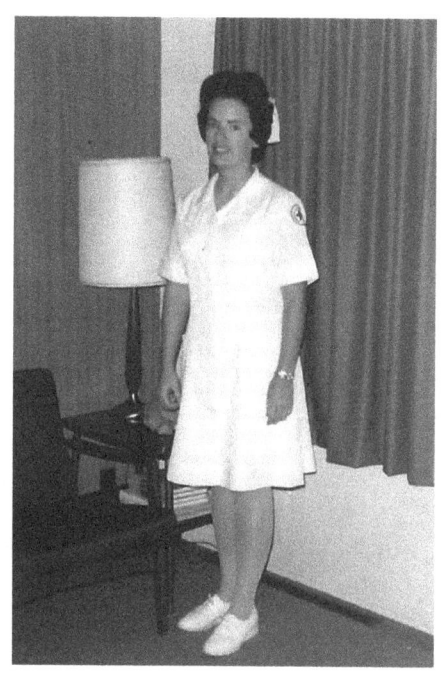

Earning her nurse's cap was a proud day for Nancy and all of us.

Mother to the World

Nancy's love and insistent personality impacted every one of her patients. "Now take these pills." "Let me fluff your pillow." "We'll just walk to the door and back." "I bet those stitches pull a lot." Lovingly but firmly, she pushed each toward recovery and healing. You just didn't say no to her. But she was there every moment along the way, encouraging, enabling, and listening carefully.

Nancy loved being an aunt. Each niece and nephew was a special gift just for her to hug and spoil and lovingly scold. She and Byron "adopted" each of their daughter Bethie's friends, following their lives with avid interest and attention. That love and concern expanded to include each child and teen in their church. Watching Nancy chat with each one was heartwarming. And that care mushroomed to surrounding teens at Kouts High School in Kouts, Indiana. Nancy and Byron had permanent seats for every basketball game, long after Bethie graduated.

Byron, Nancy and Bethie King

Loving Life

"Life—what's not to love about it?" was my sister's motto. She loved pretty stones, perky cardinals, warm tomatoes fresh from the garden. A spring breeze, fresh green beans, spring beauty flowers, and a stalwart jack-in-the-pulpit each brought her joy, which she then loved to share. A sparkle in her green eyes and the accompanying giggle warned that she was teasing and looking for fun because she loved you.

Is my Polaroid picture developing? Nancy brought light into any room she entered, but that doesn't mean she didn't understand darkness—some that she and I shared, such as cancer. Another story will help.

Terror!

The high-pitched scream of a three year old knifed through the air. This was not an often heard squeal of discovery nor a yee-haw of riding a bucking bronco. It vibrated with fear and panic and catapulted Mother to find the source. She discovered that the little girl's cry was a result of her older sister being in danger. Nancy was on fire!

I was that little girl. I was terrified for my big sister. Nancy's pants leg had caught on fire, and we were running as fast as we could toward the house for help, thus fanning the flames even more. Nancy was my guide, protector, teacher, and friend, and she was in danger!

I remember examining the scars on Nancy's leg in subsequent years. This was the first time that I remember Nancy and I sharing terror but not the last.

This story is a clear demonstration of the power of voice. Mother knew each of her children's voices and knew when and how quickly to act. Nancy's screams were heard often because life held so many exciting experiences. I must have reserved my screams to express fear.

As you read "Loving Him More," you will hear Nancy's soprano voice and, by listening, understand more about who she was and what made her tick. While it has been my voice in this introduction, soon you will be blessed to hear Nancy's heart as she shared during her last journey.

Love of vocal and instrumental music first brought Mother and Dad together, providing a foundational connection in our family. My desire in "Through Darkest Valleys" is to provide the alto for Nancy's melody as I share my own dark valley of Cancer. May our stories blend in harmony.

A Few More Details

A few more details may help prepare you to hear her love. Her words were recorded as she shared with members of her church's congregation at the weekly open mike opportunity during their worship time. When she died, a monumental task demonstrated how much Nancy was loved, as these recordings were transcribed from the audio. And we are the recipients of that love because we now have Nancy's words in print. This intense labor was simply a return of the love others received from Nancy, her husband, Byron and daughter, Bethie.

As you read, you will hear Nancy the nurse (ever teaching and explaining medical stuff), Nancy the friend (always aware of others' needs), and Nancy the child of God. May you the reader see her sunshine smile, feel her strong hug, and hear her loving heart.

Loving Him More

Nancy King's Faith and Devotions
While on Her Journey through
the Valley of the Shadow of Death

Nancy King is a woman of extraordinary faith and devotion to her Lord. This journey began on February 8, 2002, with her first cancer surgery. Those of us who were blessed to walk alongside her witnessed a rarely seen depth of love and testimony. Every Sunday that she attended worship services at Hopewell Mennonite Church, she gave us an update on her physical status as well as testimony of God working in and through her. This is a compilation of Nancy's testimonies from those services.

On April 2, 2003, Nancy and I were discussing one of the daily devotional books that she used. I said to her, "If your life were a devotional book, what would you want it to be called?" After some thought, she said, "*Loving Him More.*" And so it is that this collection of Nancy's weekly devotionals is thus titled.

Nancy went home to be with her Lord on April 30, 2003. She has left behind a wonderful legacy of love and faith. May you be blessed as you get a glimpse of her devotional life.

—Bill Beck, Pastor
Hopewell Mennonite Church
Kouts, Indiana
April 2003

Pastor Bill Beck—Picking Up the Story
FEBRUARY 10, 2002

Well, I have a prayer request and praise all wrapped up in one. Many of you may not know that Nancy King, within two weeks, has gone from thinking she had the flu to knowing she has cancer. She was in the hospital on Monday, doing tests, and she had very major surgery on Friday.

Nancy is such a wonderful, loving person, and a bunch of us were up in her room before they took her down to surgery. We had prayer, and afterward somebody asked me, "Does this ever get easy, doing this sort of thing?"

And I said, "It never really gets easier, but some people make it easier."

With some people, it's hard to encourage them, to spiritually support them in situations like this. Nancy, on the other hand, before they took her down, sat up in her bed, wagged her finger at us, and said, "I want all of you to remember that God loves me. God has been faithful to me all my life, and He's not going to stop now."

I just praise God for the wonderful testimony she is giving through this very, very difficult time that she's encountering. She had very, very extensive surgery to remove the cancer on Friday. It was a seven- or eight-hour surgery.

Byron was a little disappointed yesterday when he talked to me because he expected her to kind of bounce back more than she had. But he called early this morning and said that he got a call at home; Nancy felt good enough that she asked for a telephone to call him to ask me to remind you all to keep praying for her and to thank you all for the prayers—that she feels them.

So, she's not out of the woods yet. Keep pouring on the prayers, and God bless Nancy.

Good Morning
March 24, 2002

I just wanted to tell everybody how much I appreciate all your love and your cards and your prayers. We thought we'd try to get here for a little while today, but we're not going to be able to stay too long, so I probably won't be able to see too many of you.

But it's good to be here, and please just keep praying. The Lord's doing a pretty good job getting me ready for the next surgery, but I still need your prayers, and I appreciate all of you so very much.

—Nancy King

Thank you, Nancy. Yesterday the phone rang, and I was in the office doing my annual most unfavorite thing of the year, figuring out my taxes. I was fairly crabby, as I'm sure Timmy can attest to, and kind of growling around about having to do my taxes when you called. You probably could tell from my voice that I was kind of irritated when I first picked up the phone, but you had a lot to do about helping me change my disposition. And it was very nice to hear from you yesterday, Nancy.

—John Morgart, worship leader

Blessed beyond Description

May 26, 2002

Well, it's time for another update, folks. We got some bad news this week and some good news. I had some tests, and there's cancer back in the pancreas and in my liver. They cannot use radiation, but they are going to go ahead with the chemotherapy. It will be stronger than what we thought it would be. So, they're really going to zap me. The good news is that they've had pretty good results using the drug Gemzar.

So, I start Tuesday. It will be once a week for seven weeks at the doctor's office. Then I have one week off. They will probably do a repeat CT of the abdomen and pelvis at that time and see if it's working or not.

But I'd like to share some verses with you. The first one is in Colossians. There are so many verses in God's Word that mean so much to me. There are just a couple that I wanted to share with you. Colossians 2:6 from The Living Bible says, "And now, just as you trusted Christ to save you, trust Him, too, for each day's problems."

And that's what I've been doing and that's what I must continue to do.

And then, I wanted to read out of Psalm 112:1 followed by 6–8:

> Praise the Lord. For all who fear God and trust in Him are blessed beyond expression. Yes, happy is the man who delights in doing His commands. Such a man will not be overthrown by evil circumstances. God's constant care of him will make a deep impression on all who see it. He does not fear bad news nor live in dread of what may happen. For he is settled in his mind that Jehovah will take care of him. That is why he is not afraid, but can calmly face his foes.

And this cancer, right now, is a pretty good foe of ours. Not just mine but my family and a lot of you dear folk also. My mind isn't always calm, I have to admit, but God will not fail in providing His calmness and His peace for me.

Another very favorite verse of mine is Psalm 138:3:

> When I pray you answer me and encourage me by giving me the strength I need.

That one is underlined twice in my Bible and has been read many, many times. And then yesterday, Bethie read to me—no, it was this morning—Psalm 138:7–8:

> Though I am surrounded by troubles, you will bring me safely through them. Your power will save me. The Lord will work out His plans for my life. For Your lovingkindness, Lord, continues forever.

I don't know what God's plan is, but that's okay. I don't need to know. I know Him. What we're planning on doing now is to follow a plan of attack. We're going to keep praying, keep trusting, and we're going to try to remain positive.

And here's where I need you to help me. I need more of your prayers; I cannot tell you how much I appreciate them. I need your prayers even more now because, you know, the devil knows where I'm weak, as he knows where each of us is weak. That's where he loves to attack us.

The Lord and I talk about this quite a bit. The Lord knows where my deepest heart's desire is. He also knows that I'm His child. My body is His, and I want Him to use me, and He knows best. So, for right now, we're just going to keep a positive attitude. The Lord has given us doctors and medicine to use, and we're going to do that. We're just going to trust Him. Whatever He knows is best is what will happen.

I would ask you to please continue your prayers not only for me but for my beloved family too.

I love each of you. I thank you.

—Nancy

Playing Pac-Man
June 2, 2002

Good morning, everybody. I had my first chemo, and it went very well. And it's all your fault because you were praying for me. And I appreciate that very, very much. So keep up the prayers, and I'll keep the positive attitude.

When I was in there, getting the chemo treatment, I told Byron and Bethie I was just imagining those little Pac-Men. You remember those? They were eating the bad cancer cells. I talked to one of my other doctors early this week, and he said, "You imagine that every day." So, that's what I'm going to do, along with trust in our wonderful, wonderful Lord.

So, thank you again for all of your prayers.

Just keep it up.

—Nancy

He Alone

June 16, 2002

Good morning, everybody. I have to tell you first of all, Lila and Greg D. are in Pennsylvania visiting her mother, who had a heart attack. Lila's mother is at home and doing well as far as I know. They wanted me to mention the situation at church so that you can pray. They'll be back next week sometime.

And then, a verse sent by a friend has encouraged me this week:

> I stand silently before the Lord waiting for Him to rescue me, for salvation comes from Him alone. Yes, He alone is my rock, my rescuer, defense and fortress. Why then, should I be tense [and I'm adding "or afraid"] with fear when troubles come? (Psalm 62:1–2 TLB)

Another friend gave me a song. It's in our blue hymnal books, so you can look it up for yourself too. But I want to read part of it to you:

> God will make a way.
> Where there seems to be no way.
> He works in ways we cannot see.
> He will make a way for me.
> He will be my guide,
> Hold me closely to His side.
> With love and strength for each new day.
> He will make a way.
>
> ("God Will Make a Way" by Don Moen, ©1990 Integrity Music)

And, I'm doing fine. This week we have a repeat blood test called CA19-9. Last time they did it, my count was five thousand. Normal is forty. So, we're hoping that the chemo is helping.

Also, if you would please keep in your prayers that the Lord would keep my blood work up high enough, my platelets especially, because if they fall below a certain level, I can't have any more chemo. Now they're at 102,000, and if they drop to fifty thousand, I can't have any more chemo. So, I need you to ask the Lord, if it's okay, keep that up high too. Otherwise I'm doing very well, and the Lord is working in my heart and in my life, I know.

I thank you again for all your prayers.

—Nancy

Come and See

June 23, 2002

Well, good morning, again, everyone. I have a couple verses to share with you today. The first one is Psalm 50:14–15:

> What I want from you is your true thanks. I want your promises fulfilled. I want you to trust me in your times of trouble, so I can rescue you and you can give me glory.

Then also Psalm 66:5:

> Come, see the glorious things God has done. What marvelous miracles happen to His people.

We have two huge praises today. This last week, I had my blood work done on Monday. The week before, my platelet count was 102,000, and I was a little concerned. If it drops below fifty thousand, they won't give me my chemo treatment. I was afraid that maybe it would be lower, so I asked you last week to pray for the platelet count. This week it was 166,000. And so we were very, very thankful for that.

Then I also had another CA 19-9 test. The one I had when they found the cancer had returned was over 5,200. This time it was five hundred. So, we're very thankful.

Praise the Lord!

—Nancy

Promises Fulfilled

June 30, 2002

Good morning, again, everyone. It's good to be here again; good to see all of you. The verse I have for today is in 2 Timothy 2:13, again reading out of The Living Bible. You know, all of us have different things in our lives that kind of weigh us down sometimes and get us discouraged. Sometimes we feel like we can't even pray anymore; we can't even say, "Dear Lord."

This verse spoke so firmly to me, and I want to share it with you:

> Even when we are too weak to have any faith left, He remains faithful to us and will help us, for He cannot disown us who are part of Himself and He will always carry out His promises to us." (2 Timothy 2:13 TLB)

And I am so very thankful for that. A prayer request I have, again, is for platelets. My platelet count was down a bit last week, but hopefully it will be okay this week and I can have my full treatment. I have one more this week, and then I get a week off. At that time, they'll probably do another CT scan and see what's going on inside me. So, if you'd ask the Lord to keep my platelets up for a couple more weeks so we can get the full treatments in, I'd appreciate it.

Thank you all very much.

—Nancy

Kindness and Faithfulness

July 7, 2002

Good morning, again, everyone. The verse I want to read today is Psalm 92:1–2:

> It is good to say thank you to the Lord, to sing praises to the God who is above all gods. Every morning tell Him, "Thank you for Your kindness" and every evening rejoice in all His faithfulness.

I also rejoice in your faithfulness because you folks were praying again last week. My platelets went up from 118,00 to 221,000. And that is amazing. Even the girl that gives me my chemo said it was due to prayer. So, I just want to thank you and encourage you for all your prayers. It means so much to me (and to our friend Marlin too, I know) and lots of other people that you keep in your prayers. So don't ever quit, because we all need you so much.

Thank you, and God bless each of you.

—Nancy

I Will Sing
July 21, 2002

Good morning, everybody. It's good to be back in church again today. My whole week was messed up last Sunday because we had to be at the hospital for a while. I got home Thursday night, and I'm doing well. I just wanted to thank you again for all your prayers. And while we were there, I had another CA 19-9 blood test (the one that was initially so high and then was down to five hundred last time). This time it was ninety-three! So, we're very, very thankful for that. I had a CT scan of the abdomen and pelvis Thursday night, and we don't know the results of that yet. We'll probably find out Tuesday.

Here are a couple verses I wanted to share with you:

> Oh, how grateful and thankful I am to the Lord because He is so good. I will sing praise to the name of the Lord who is above all lords. (Psalm 7:17 TLB)

And I know too that there are things that some of you have that are hurting right now, and I just wanted to read another verse just for that. This is Psalm 9:9–10:

> All who are oppressed may come to Him. He is a refuge for them in their times of trouble. All those who know your mercy, Lord, will count on you for help. For you have never yet forsaken those who trust in you.

No matter what we're going through—if it's joys—God's happy to hear our praise of that. And when it's sorrows or unhappy things or hard times, God will never, ever, ever leave us.

—Nancy

Good News
July 28, 2002

Good morning, again, everyone. I just wanted to tell you again how wonderful you all are in praying for me. We received some very good news this last week. The results of the CT scan, and now, if I get it straight here, showed that there was no visual evidence of cancer in the liver or the pancreas. So, we're very, very thankful. That doesn't mean there's not some microscopic cancer there, so we are going to go ahead and continue the treatments. But I am only scheduled to have three. One a week, and then I get a week off, instead of seven in a row. So, I'm looking forward to only three.

And today, the first verse I found to share with you is Psalm 9:1–2:

> Oh, Lord, I will praise you with all my heart and tell everyone about the marvelous things you do. I will be glad. Yes, filled with joy because of you.

Because we do still have some heartaches here and some concerns, I found Psalm 46:1:

> God is our refuge and strength, A tested help in times of trouble.

We don't have to wonder if He is going to help us. He is a tested help. One more, Matthew 6:34:

> So don't be anxious about tomorrow. God will take care of your tomorrow, too.
> Live one day at a time.

Thank you again everyone, for your prayers, and I ask you please to keep them up. I love you all.

—Nancy

Worthy of Trust
August 4, 2002

Good morning, everyone. I wanted to thank you, again, for all your prayers. This Wednesday I'll have my other port put back in just as an outpatient. Then they won't have to stick me in the arm all the time for my chemo. I'm looking forward to that relief.

You know, there are a lot of times we don't understand why things happen. I had the privilege of knowing Uriah. And yes, we still miss him. I don't know God's plan for letting Marlin go home (too soon we think), but in reading God's Word this week, He gave me a couple of verses, and I just wanted to share them with you.

> For all God's words are right, and everything He does
> is worthy of our trust. (Psalm 33:4 TLB)

Even if we don't understand it, all things that He does and allows are worthy of our trust. And I really like Psalm 29:11:

> He will give His people strength. He will bless them
> with peace.

And God will do this. He has done it already for a lot of us. And He will continue to give us His strength and His peace. Just rely on Him and trust Him like Chris was talking about last week. All things that God does are worthy of our trust. And He will give peace and strength.

—Nancy

Collecting Tears
August 11, 2002

Good morning, everybody. I had my port put in, so I get a vacation this next week, and I'm almost raring to go to have my chemo through my port the following week. I am very thankful to have the port so that they don't have to stick me every time. I appreciate that.

And while I've been reading this week, the Lord brought a couple of verses to me that I'd like to share with you. We've had a few tears this week, and that's okay, because God himself even had tears. So, it's okay if we do too. It helps to clean our eyes out.

Psalm 56:8 is a really comforting verse:

> You have seen me tossing and turning through the night. You have collected all my tears and preserved them in Your bottle. You have recorded every one in Your book.

Note, it says not just one, not just two, but all of them. God is with us and knows when we cry and is right there to comfort us. And then, a verse I shared with you before but is still a special one—Psalm 138:3.

> When I pray, you answer me and encourage me by giving me the strength I need.

And yes, Sandra, we are continuing to pray for you and the whole family. And I appreciate everybody's prayers coming our way too. We love you all.

—Nancy

Blessed Strength and Peace
August 18, 2002

Good morning, everybody. I have a prayer request, not my own but for a friend named Marilyn. She's undergoing some tests, so please remember her in prayer.

I had a CA 19-9 Friday. I won't know the results until Tuesday. We have a conference Tuesday before my chemo.

This week has been a busy week. It was Bethie's last week home. She left yesterday, returning to college for her senior year. A verse the Lord gave me earlier in the week and again yesterday is Psalm 29:11. This again is in The Living Bible:

> He will give His people strength. He will bless them with peace.

And I'm claiming this because it's going to be really different without Bethie around. Thank you.

—Nancy

Thank You
August 25, 2002

Good morning again, everyone. We had some good news this week. I had my CA 19-9 blood test that tells how much cancer's in my body. About a month ago, it was ninety-three. This time it was sixty-eight. So, we're very, very thankful for that. I want to share with you from Psalm 92. I read it before, but I think it's worth reading again. Psalm 92:1–2:

> It is good to say thank you to the Lord. To sing praises to the God who is above all gods. Every morning tell Him, "Thank you for Your kindness" and every evening rejoice in all His faithfulness.

And you know, with the good news that we got this week, you would have thought that I would have been a very happy person (especially on Tuesday and Wednesday), but, you know, I wasn't. The devil (the enemy / Satan / father of lies) was just having a heyday, and he was making me worry. Even before we got to the doctor's office on Tuesday, I was worrying. *What if my blood test is up?* And so I had kind of a struggle for a while. Finally, the Lord got through to me that I should trust Him more because He is so wonderful and He loves me so much. And He's so wise and all-powerful, and so I should just trust Him more with everything that concerns me. I want to leave you with another verse, Colossians 2:6.

> And now, just as you trusted Christ to save you, trust Him, too, for each day's problems.

And please continue to pray for my platelet count to stay up so I can have my treatments. Continue to pray for that, and if you don't mind, you can pray too that I can remember to tell the devil where to go.

—Nancy

Filled with Joy
September 1, 2002

I'm Nancy. I think most of you know that, but I wanted to say good morning again. And I just want to thank the Lord for each one of you today. I do it all the time anyway, but your prayers you will never know how much your prayers mean to me and to my family. And I just wanted to tell you again, thank you.

My platelet count this week was 263,000 (up from 135,000). And that's very good, and I'm very thankful. Keep up the good work, everyone. I want to share Psalm 9:1–2:

> Oh, Lord, I will praise you with all my heart and tell everyone about the marvelous things You do. I will be glad, yes, filled with joy because of You.

And because of each of you also.

Stop to Listen
September 15, 2002

Good morning. It's Nancy again. I just want to encourage each of you to ... well, this week I was talking to the Lord, and sometimes I get so busy I don't listen to what He's trying to tell me. A verse He gave me this week is Isaiah 30:15:

In quietness and in confidence shall be your strength.

And I think He was trying to tell me to take time to listen to Him once in a while. It's really important that we all take time to listen to what God's trying to tell us. He loves us so much and wants to communicate with us. If we're the ones who are doing the talking all the time, how's He going to get through to us? So, I'm trying to practice that.

Oh, I forgot to tell you, I had a CA 19-9 drawn Friday. I will get the results Monday or Tuesday. And thank you again for all your prayers and your cards and everything. I appreciate it.

Tell God Your Needs
SEPTEMBER 29, 2002

This is Nancy King, and I'm glad to be here today. I'm feeling much better today, thank you, and thank you for all your prayers. I think I was trying to get the flu last week, but I'm doing fine now. My platelet count this week was 275,000, which is very good, and I'm very thankful. I had a CA 19-9 two weeks ago and—don't be worried, but it was a little elevated. The doctor said that it's nothing to worry about because it does that sometimes. So that's the thought that we're going with. And I won't have the next one for two weeks yet. So, it's kind of a long month, but that's okay because we've got the Lord to trust, and He's been so faithful. And even though we as humans sometimes worry—our thoughts get going every which way, and we like to worry a lot. Even if we don't like to worry, we still do.

But the Lord reminded me again of two very familiar verses. You know, sometimes we just read them and don't really think about what we're reading, but I had to really think this time because I was worrying. Philippians 4:6–7:

> Don't worry about anything. [Now, that's a big sentence right there all by itself.] Instead, pray about everything. Tell God your needs and don't forget to thank Him for His answers. [Sometimes, I forget that.] If you do this, [and here's a great, great, great promise that He has given us, and you know His promises are true] you will experience God's peace which is far more wonderful than the human mind can understand. His peace will keep your thoughts [those that like to get away from me sometimes] and your hearts quiet and at rest as you trust in Christ Jesus.

And He'll do the same for you anytime you ask Him.

He Gives Strength
October 6, 2002

Good morning, everyone. As some of you may notice, I have my real hair back again. Wigs are nice, but I like my own hair. So, you'll probably be seeing me in it some more.

Today I want to share some encouragement God gave me this week. It is from a little book called *God Calling* by A.J. Russell. It is written as God just talking to us. This part is called "Wisdom."

> "As thy days, so shall thy strength be." And then, God is saying to us, "I have promised that for every day you live, the strength shall be given you. Do not fear. Face each difficulty, sure that the wisdom and strength will be given you for it. Claim it. Rely on me to keep my promise about this. In my universe, for every task I give one of my children, there is set aside all that is necessary for its performance. So, why fear? So, why doubt?"

How thankful I am that He does give us the strength.

—Nancy

Sing Praise

October 12, 2002

This is Nancy again, and I just wanted to share with you how wonderful our Lord is. I had a CA 19-9 on Friday and won't know the results until Tuesday. But that doesn't matter because it's all in the Lord's hands.

And I've been reading again in the psalms where the writer talks about our God treasuring us humans. Thinking about the sunrises and the sunsets and the stars and His creation, how wonderful they are and how wonderful He is. We have a wonderful God who still takes time to love us. And I am so very thankful.

So, I'm going to read Psalm 7:17 this morning from my Living Bible:

> Oh how grateful and thankful I am to the Lord because
> He is so good. I will sing praise to the name of the Lord
> Who is above all lords.

He is so wonderful, and I'm just so thankful.

Draw Closer
October 20, 2002

This is Nancy King. I have a couple of things this morning. Craig and Beth, speaking for Byron and myself, we love you all very much, and you're always welcome in our home or here in our church. And we will be praying for you. And thank you for all you've done for us and for our church. We appreciate it.

Secondly, Bob and Phyllis E. live next to us. Bob's sister has been diagnosed with liver cancer. She'll be going to Chicago this week for consultation, and they're not exactly sure what all they're going to do, but if you'd please pray for Marilyn, we'd appreciate it.

And I want to thank you again for all your prayers for me. This week we found out that my CA 19-9 was a bit elevated. They say not to worry about it, but I did. And again, I had to tell the devil where to go—a couple different times. I want to let you know how wonderful God's peace is. And He will give it to us. And I appreciate it so much because I couldn't go this road without you folks, my family, and most of all, our God.

I was reading in James this week, so I'm going to read to you:

> So give yourselves humbly to God. Resist the devil and
> he will flee from you. (James 4:7 TLB)

Because we're God's children, the devil has to go when we tell him in God's name to leave us alone. He has to go, and he did. That doesn't mean he won't come back, but he has to go. And verse 8:

> And when you draw nigh to God, God will draw close
> to you. (James 4:8 TLB)

And I'm so very thankful that He does that for all of us.

Finding Refuge

NOVEMBER 10, 2002

This is Nancy King, and good morning, everyone. This has been my week off, but I've been awful tired this week. And it seems like when I get tired, my voice goes. So I'm sorry. I hope you can hear me all right.

In reading this week, I was in psalms again, which is one of my favorite places. I came across some verses that tell us what our God is like. And I just thought I'd share them with you.

> Your steadfast love, Oh lord, is as great as all the heavens. Your faithfulness reaches beyond the clouds. Your justice is as solid as God's mountains. Your decisions are as full of wisdom as the oceans are with water. You are concerned with men and animals alike. How precious is Your constant love, Oh God! All humanity takes refuge in the shadow of Your wings. (Psalm 36:5–7 TLB)

What a wonderful God we have.

One Day at a Time
November 17, 2002

Good morning. I'm Nancy, and I too want to thank the Lord for the music ensemble that we enjoyed this morning. It was very nice, and I appreciate them all.

I had a CA 19-9 last week. The results this week showed it to be up again a little bit, but we have decided not to worry about it, and I don't want any of you to worry about it because God is the only one that knows what's going on inside my body. And I would rather trust God and His wisdom than the wisdom of the doctors. Not because they're bad doctors but just because I trust the Lord a little bit more.

Verses from Matthew 6 were brought to me Tuesday morning, before I even found out about the blood test results. Matthew 6:8:

> Remember your Father knows exactly what you need even before you ask Him.

And then Matthew 6:34:

> So don't be anxious about tomorrow. God will take care of your tomorrow, too. Live one day at a time.

And I think that's good not only for me and my family but for each one of us. Remember, God knows what we need. So, it may not always be what we want, but He knows what we need. Don't hesitate to talk to Him about it. And then be faithful and trust Him.

Really, Really Big

DECEMBER 1, 2002

Good morning. It's Nancy, again. This week my platelets were down a little bit, so I didn't get quite all my treatment, but I got three-fourths of it. I'm thankful for that and that this next week is my week off—a vacation. I'm really looking forward to that too.

I have something that I would like for you to do, please. I would like you to picture in your mind the very biggest, biggest, biggest thing you can ever imagine; bigger than elephants, bigger than the Empire State Building. Think of something really, really big. Now I want to read to you what is my prayer for all of us. It's in Ephesians 3:17–20:

> And I pray that Christ will be more and more at home in your hearts, living within you as you trust in Him. May your roots go down deep into the soil of God's marvelous love and may you be able to feel and understand, as all God's children should, how long, how wide, how deep and how high His love really is; and to experience this love for yourselves, though it is so great that you will never see the end of it or fully know or understand it. And so, at last you will be filled up with God, Himself.
>
> I think that's one of our goals—to be filled up with God so that His love just flows out from us to others.
>
> Now glory be to God, who by His mighty power at work within us, is able to do far more than we would ever dare to ask or even dream of, infinitely beyond our highest prayers, desires, thoughts or hope. (Ephesians 3:20 TLB)

What a marvelous and wonderful God we have.

Crowns

DECEMBER 8, 2002

Good morning, everyone. It's Nancy again. This week I've been doing some thinking—believe it or not. I've been thinking about our wonderful Lord, our almighty God. And you know, I was just thinking about how great He is. I have trouble talking to two people at one time, but God is with each one of us—so many, many, many people. He's with all of us all of the time, and that just boggles my mind. And I'm just very thankful that He is with all of us. I told a friend of mine I plan to ask the Lord how He does that when I get to heaven, but by the time I get there, it really won't matter. So, I'll just be thankful for it while I'm down here on earth.

I was reading Psalm 8:3–5:

> When I look up into the night skies and see the work of your fingers—the moon and the stars You have made—I cannot understand how You can bother with mere puny man, to pay any attention to him. And yet you have made him only a little lower than the angels and placed a crown of glory and honor upon his head.

And I'm just so thankful that He's with us all the time ... all of us ... all the time. Amen.

Comforting Hugs
December 15, 2002

It's Nancy again. As most of you know me, you know I like hugs. And God gave me a hug this week. And I'd like to share it with you because it's for you too.

> What a wonderful God we have—He is the Father of our Lord Jesus Christ, the source of every mercy and the One Who so wonderfully comforts and strengthens us in all our hardships and trials. And why does He do this? So that when others are troubled, needing our sympathy and encouragement, we can pass on to them this same help and comfort God has given us. (2 Corinthians 1:3–4 TLB)

And I'm so thankful for that. It was just like a big hug.

Distractions

DECEMBER 22, 2002

Good morning. It's Nancy again. I have an extra request. Byron and I were watching the basketball game between Andrean and Griffith last night. During the part we happened to see, a young man named Dan M. was injured. His head injury didn't look good at all. Please remember him in prayer.

You know, it may be hard to believe, but I do get busy sometimes. Then it is easy to forget what my priorities should be. The Lord gave me a verse this week that kind of made me sit back and remember what those priorities should be.

I'm reading Colossians 4:2 today: "Don't be weary in prayer."

Sometimes I read my other devotional books, and then I fall asleep or I get busy and I don't pray. Prayer is just talking to my beloved God. Additionally, I thought that if Byron and Bethie or others didn't talk to me ... they just assumed I knew they loved me ... that would be kind of hard. I do know they love me, but it's always nice to talk with them too. So, the Lord just really said, "Don't forget me."

> Don't be weary in prayer; keep at it; watch for God's answers, and remember to be thankful when they come. (Colossians 4:2 TLB)

Because they will come, no matter whether we see them or not. God loves us so much, and He will answer our prayers.

Thank you.

Glorious Blessings
December 29, 2002

This is Nancy again. I have a really big praise today because this week I got to go up to South Beloit near Wisconsin to our Wilson family reunion. It was tiring, but we made it, and we had a wonderful time. We visited with a lot of my nieces and nephews and my brothers and sisters, and it was a really wonderful time.

And I just want to also praise the Lord for each one of you and the blessing you are to our family—your prayers, your love, your cards, food that's brought sometimes, and other things that you do for us. It just means so much to know that you're praying. That's one reason I made it so well this last week. And I appreciate it; we all do—a lot.

I'm going to read Psalm 103:1–2:

> I bless the holy name of God with all my heart. Yes, I
> will bless the Lord and not forget the glorious things
> He does for me.

And you all are some of the wonderful things He does for us. One other thing I forgot to thank you for is your singing. I can't sing very well anymore, which I really miss a lot. But I'm singing in my heart along with you, and I appreciate listening to all of you sing.

Good, Not Evil
January 5, 2003

This is Nancy again, and good morning, everyone. I'd like to read for you this morning a little devotional from *Grace for the Moment* by Max Lucado. The thoughts are called "Don't Miss God's Answer" and are based on Genesis 18:14:

> Is anything too hard for the Lord? No! The God of surprises strikes again. God does that for the faithful. Just when the womb gets too old for babies, Sarah gets pregnant. Just when the failure is too great for grace, David is pardoned. The lesson ... three words ... don't give up! Is the road long? Don't stop. Is the night black? Don't quit. God is watching. For all you know, right at this moment the check may be in the mail, the apology may be in the making, the job contract may be on the desk. Don't quit! For if you do, you may miss the answers to your prayers.

And then I wanted to read Jeremiah 29:11–13:

> "For I know the plans I have for you," says the Lord. "They are plans for good and not for evil, to give you a future and a hope. When you pray, I will listen. You will find me when you seek Me, if you look for Me in earnest."

And how very thankful I am that even with the coming of the new year, we can rest in God, that we know He has every day in control, so we don't have to worry about it. Amen.

He Knows and Understands
January 12, 2003

Good morning, everyone. This is Nancy again. As I was reading my devotions this week, the Lord brought a verse to me. Sometimes I have trouble comprehending things. For instance, it's sometimes hard for me to understand how God could love me and how He could love me so much! It really boggles my mind to think about and really understand God loving me and that He never goes away from me. He's always right there by me, just waiting for me to say, "Okay, Lord. I need your help here," or, "I need your help there," and He's always ready to give it to me. Sometimes I get busy, and I forget to ask Him or mention it to Him. And so, when I read this verse, it was kind of special. This is Hebrews 2:18:

> For since He Himself has now been through suffering and temptation, He knows what it is like when we suffer and are tempted and He is wonderfully able to help us.

No matter what we go through—it doesn't matter if it is temptation, and we know there is a whole lot of that out in the word today—or if it's a little bit of not feeling too good, or like Bill had the flu, God is right there just waiting to help us. All we have to do is ask Him, and He's always faithful.

And I'm very thankful for that.

Finding Perfect Peace
January 19, 2003

Good morning, everyone. It's Nancy again. A couple weeks ago, we had our conference with the doctor. My CA 19-9, the blood test that supposedly tells how much cancer is in my body, had gone from 188 to 284. So, it's going the wrong way. But we're not going to worry about it because God knows what's going on inside my body. We trust God to take care of what's there, and it's His will. But I just wanted to keep you informed of what's happening with me.

I wanted to also thank you very, very much again for everyone's prayers and for the note that someone left in our mailbox today. It was very nice.

I wanted to share with you Isaiah 26:3–4:

> He will keep in perfect peace all those who trust in Him, whose thoughts turn often to the Lord. Trust in the Lord God always, for in the Lord Jehovah is your everlasting strength.

I like the everlasting part because I seem to run out of strength sometimes. But the verse isn't only for me. It's for each of you also.

Always Watching
January 26, 2003

Good morning, everyone. It's Nancy, again. First, I have a prayer request. We heard earlier this week that Denise's mother was in the hospital and is not doing very well. Rod and Denise are in Denver this weekend for a funeral. They'll be back sometime today, and then I imagine they'll want to go down and see her mom, Ruby. Please remember Rod and Denise at this time.

I want to thank you all again for your prayers for me and for my family. I have struggled this week and then was reminded that this is the devil's work in me—making me discouraged. So then I had to have a long talk with the Lord and also had to tell the devil (the enemy / Satan / father of lies) where to go again.

You know, I just wish he would listen to me and stay away when I tell him the first time. But he doesn't do that. But he had to leave because I'm God's child, and by the power given to me by God through the blood of our Lord Jesus Christ, the devil cannot stay and bug me.

And so I just want to encourage you all that when he bugs you—because he will, if he hasn't already (I'm sure he has because he doesn't like us to love our Lord)—just tell him where to go. He may not stay away very long, but he has to go right then and there. So, just do it, and he'll go.

Discouragement leaves me feeling empty. I appreciate the songs this morning. And I want to thank you, Don, for the reading you shared this morning. That was very good.

So I asked the Lord to fill me up again, because I have been pretty close to empty. And the Lord gave me some verses that I want to share with you. This is 1 Peter 5:7–9 from The Living Bible:

> Let Him have all your worries and cares, for He is always thinking about you and watching everything that concerns you. Be careful—watch out for attacks from Satan, your great enemy. He prowls around like a hungry, roaring lion, looking for some victim to tear

apart. Stand firm when he attacks. Trust the Lord; and remember that other Christians all around the world are going through these sufferings, too.

Again, just remember to give God your worries and your cares. He is always thinking about you and watching.
　　He loves you.

—Nancy

Thankful Hearts
February 2, 2003

Good morning, everyone. This is Nancy again. I want to thank the Lord for this day and that we can all be here together. I appreciate that. The verse I found this week that made me stop and do some more thinking was Psalm 95:2: "Come before Him with thankful hearts."

Sometimes when I'm having my devotions, I've got so much that I need to talk to Him about that I forget to thank Him for things. And then when I do thank Him sometimes, I just list the usual things.

As I was thinking about it a little more this week, I realized that I am very thankful for the unusual things too—like unanswered prayer. Sometimes we think we know what's best for us and ask for that or tell God what He should do. And sometimes that's not what's best. So at times we need to thank God for unanswered prayer.

I need to thank Him more for the deep down inside things like when He never turns away from me no matter how many times I fail Him. I'm so thankful for that. And even when the devil makes me feel like I'm all alone, I'm not. God is there. I need to be more thankful for that.

There are so many things that I forget to thank Him for ... like I said—the deep down inside things that I don't always think about. And one of the things I'm very thankful for is each one of you and your love for Him, your love for us. We appreciate it very much and thank you for all your prayers. It means so much. We just love you all.

Don't Worry about Me
February 9, 2003

Good morning, everyone. It's Nancy again.

One thing I'm very, very, very, very, very thankful for today is that last year at this time, I was in intensive care ... and I'm here in church today. I appreciate that. I'd rather be in church any day than in intensive care. But I am also thankful for the year God has given us and for all the blessings He has given us.

Before I forget, I want to tell you that the boxes you guys sent to the college students are definitely appreciated. Bethie and Mary both got their boxes and invaded them promptly. They are really appreciated.

I want to share Psalm 29:11 with you:

> He will give His people strength. He will bless them
> with peace.

This week was conference time again. My platelets were up, which is good. They were 135,000, so I got my full treatment. But my cancer marker number was also up. It jumped from 284 in January to 1,094 this time. But, as this verse says, "He will give HIs people strength.

> He will bless them with peace" (Psalm 29:11 TLB).

God is the only one who knows what's going on inside my body. I'd rather trust God than the doctors any day.

I don't want you folks to worry about me. Just keep praying. I know you do, and I appreciate that. Just keep trusting the Lord because He knows what's going on.

On the way to church this morning, we were listening to the radio. I don't even know the preacher's name. He was talking about the plans we make and how we ask God to bless our plans. He then said something that was interesting. He said we should have God plan our blessings. He went on to say that if we're in God's will, God is definitely planning our blessings. If we're in His plan, then He will plan our blessings.

We don't have to worry about anything else then. He's in control, and He knows what's going on. So, I just wanted to share that with you.

And thank you again for all your prayers.

We appreciate it.

God Is Real, God Is Good
February 16, 2003

This is Nancy again. I just wanted to say good morning to everybody and let you know what's happening. We went to see Dr. N on Thursday. When he felt around on my belly where I've been having a little bit of pain, he felt a firmness there. So, I'm going to have a CT scan on Monday. I haven't had one since July, so it's about time. He gave me a little bit of medicine for the pain. It's helped a lot, so I can rest better at night; I'm thankful for that.

When I was reading my devotions this week, I have to confess that I read ahead a day. (Sometimes I do that.) This is from *Grace for the Moment* by Max Lucado—"God's Help is Near."

> Hebrews 11:1 says, "Faith means being sure of the things we hope for and knowing that something is real even if we do not see it." Faith is the belief that God is real and that God is good. It is a choice to believe that that One Who made it all hasn't left it all and that He still sends light into the shadows and responds to gestures of faith. Faith is the belief that God will do what is right. [I like that saying. It is a good one.] God says that the more hopeless your circumstances, the more likely your salvation. The greater your cares, the more genuine your prayers. The darker the room, the greater the need for light. God's help is near and always available. But, it is only given to those who seek it.

And how wonderful it is that God's help is always available no matter where we are or what our circumstances might be. God is faithful. Amen.

Making It Through
March 2, 2003

Well, good morning, everyone. This is Nancy again. We had some results from the CT scan this last week. The pancreas and the lymph nodes look pretty good, but there are more spots on the liver. So there's some involvement there again. I've had a little trouble with nausea and some vomiting this week. So I need your prayers to continue.

Please pray that the Lord will give me strength and that He'll be with me throughout all this. I'd like to read Philippians 4:13 out of my Living Bible:

> I can do everything God asks me to do with the help
> of Christ Who gives me the strength and the power.

Sometimes that's the only way that we can make it. We can be sure that He will give us all that we need.

We Will Rejoice
March 9, 2003

Good morning, everyone. It's Nancy again. Thank you for your prayers this last week. I've had a better week, and I appreciate it very much.

I just wanted to tell Brenna to hang in there, kiddo. The Lord is good. He loves you so much. If you just keep turning to Him with your questions and your problems and all, He will help you.

He'll guide you in the right path, and you'll be happier than you can ever believe. So, just hang in there, and that's not just for Brenna either. That's for all you kids in high school and other schools who are having problems and questions. You just hang on to the Lord, and you'll do fine.

I am reading Psalm 118:24:

> This is the day that the Lord has made. We will rejoice
> and be glad in it.

And we can all just stop and begin by thinking about ten things that we have to be thankful for, things that God has helped us with or given us.

What a wonderful treasure we have, our wonderful Lord.

A Message Relayed
March 16, 2003

Good morning. Nancy couldn't be here this morning, and she wanted me to share a few things with you. She said don't worry about her; she appreciates your cards and your love, and, Lord willing, she'll be here next Sunday.

She said she loves all of you, and she's praying for us also. That's sweet of her. She just keeps praying for everyone else. She wants me to read Matthew 6:34 (NIV):

> Therefore, do not worry about tomorrow, for tomorrow will worry about itself.
> Each day has enough trouble of its own.

—Lila D.

I Am Not Afraid
March 23, 2003

This is Nancy again, and I just wanted to say good morning to everybody. I'm glad to be here again this Sunday. Most of you know by now that we have chosen to not have any more chemo. The doctors said the chemo wasn't working anymore and gave us a choice. We could either take it even though it wasn't helping, or we could stop it. We decided to stop it. So, that's where we stand right now. The rest is totally up to the Lord.

I just wanted to leave you with Hebrews 13:5b–6 (TLB):

> For God has said, "I will never, never fail you nor forsake you." That is why we can say without any doubt or fear, "The Lord is my helper and I am not afraid of anything that mere man can do to me."

I don't want you to be afraid of anything. Just keep trusting the Lord and keep praying. And I thank you all for your prayers and your cards and all the love that you continue to give to all.

He Will Never Fail Us
April 6, 2003

Good morning, everyone. We're glad to be here today. I wasn't real sure I was going to make it, but we did ... a little bit late.

I just want to read Hebrews 13:5b again. I know I read it last week, but it still is all true:

> For God has said, "I will never, never fail you nor forsake you."

I just wanted to remind you all that no matter what happens, God is right there beside us, and He will never fail us. So, as long as you have God, you can handle anything.

—Nancy

Through Darkest Valleys

Rebecca Kordatzky Singing Alto

Gently Rolling Hills

Hello, friend. I am honored by your presence. Do you hear the breeze whispering to us? "Come! Follow me; enjoy the mild weather and ever-so-pleasant view along these gently rolling hills." And your company is the beautiful bow atop this gorgeous day. The pathway is so much more enjoyable with you along to visit. Another pair of eyes is always welcome. Let's follow advice from the father of our national parks, John Muir, as he spoke about hiking. He said, "I don't like either the word or the thing. People ought to saunter in the mountains—not hike!" So, today we saunter.

I have had the privilege of being on life's journey for many decades. Of course, on any worthwhile trip, one must expect twists and turns, even learning to embrace the ups and downs.

Writing this story has been a new journey for me. In the beginning, I envisioned this to simply be an editing project. I wanted to honor my sister and her legacy of faith and planned to edit her reflections. I would need to write a short introduction and perhaps a brief afterword. Not too big of a project, right?

But I must now admit that this simply-editing project has demanded more. I realized that I owe it to you, my fellow traveler, to share other parts of the story, including some of those twists, turns, ups, and downs that have been part of my journey.

I packed a lunch—fresh fruit, cheese, and crisp bagels. Shall we stop by this brook and enjoy its music while we have lunch?

My dream home will have just such a happy, bubbling brook across the back corner of the wooded lot. It will be the perfect stream in which to discover crawdads and to create small dams.

<hr />

I have learned that a critical component of happiness is being able to see the beauty along the way and being able to laugh at my many foibles. Some days I just shake my head in disbelief over the contradictions that slip out of my mouth and display themselves blatantly to everyone around. Some contradictions are frightening, but many times, I just have to laugh as well.

Take poetry, for example. I taught English and literature, but I must admit there is a lot of poetry that I don't understand. I even admitted that fact to my students (while assigning them a fairly extensive poetry project). Secretly, I wondered when the literacy police would come knocking on my door. But saying it gave me freedom to explore why I felt that way. Do I really hate it?

Not at all. I love poetry that speaks to me. The challenge of using just a few words to convey an amazing idea or feeling calls deeply to my inner wordsmith. Take for example, Carl Sandburg's poem "Fog": "The fog comes on little cat feet. It sits looking over harbor and city on silent haunches and then moves on." Those twenty-one words create a flying carpet, capable of taking the reader to many different times and places.

As I thought further back into my relationship with poetry, I realized that the poetry of King David in the Bible has resonated with me for multiple decades. I find freedom in David's poetry—freedom to be sad, happy, depressed, elated, angry, reflective, grateful.

Psalm 23 is one of the best known of the one hundred and fifty psalms. Initially, it was used by ancient Hebrews in their worship but now is read, recited, and sung by people the world over. Of course, I grew up reciting the King James Version—which I love. But I also appreciate many of the more current translations that broaden my understanding. This is from the New Living Translation:

> The Lord is my Shepherd; I have all that I need.
> He lets me rest in green meadows;
> He leads me beside peaceful streams.
> He renews my strength.
> He guides me along right paths, bringing honor to his name.
> Even when I walk through the darkest valley,
> I will not be afraid, for you are close beside me.
> Your rod and your staff protect and comfort me.
> You prepare a feast for me in the presence of my enemies.
> You honor me by anointing my head with oil.
> My cup overflows with blessings.
> Surely your goodness and unfailing love will pursue me
> all the days of my life,
> and I will live in the house of the Lord forever.

To me, this means that the holy, just, and loving God that I see in nature, creation, and people and whom I read about in the Bible personally looks after me because I agree that someone should and I have asked Him to handle that not-so-small task. In His care, I can rest confidently and be content. He provides what I need, although not always what I want. When I turn to Him, He brings refreshment, peace, and joy. He shows me the path to blessing because He promised to do that, and He cannot be false to His promises. He cannot break His word.

Even when I experience dark times, I do not need to fear because He has promised to be with me always. He continually provides the comfort I need and takes care of me right in front of those who would rejoice at my failures. He shows that I am special to him and my life is overflowing with gifts and blessings. His mercy and love are with me always, and He plans for me to be with Him always. But I must trust Him enough to look for those blessings, to peek around to discover His mercy and love.

That was a delightful lunch. Let's walk a bit and work the kinks out. Here is a well-marked pathway; we can relax, knowing the way is clear.

Look at that tall bee balm beckoning, "Come this way." And what a beautiful gray rock—smoothed by buffeting rain and warmed by the midday sun—a perfect perch. Perhaps we will see some bees or even a hummingbird searching the deep red flowers for an afternoon snack.

Different from our leisurely stroll today, I have wandered in dark valleys. I remember often fighting panic, trying to figure out how to fix a crisis. I can be like the young child who refused to sit down in church. Finally, after Mother's urging and cajoling, the child does comply but loudly declares, "My inside is standing."

Yes, my two-year-old self does enjoy a stubborn streak or a temper tantrum now and then. Sometimes I am so intent on solving problems that I wear myself out running in circles. Exhausted, I finally admit, "I need help." So, where does one turn for help in a crisis?

Isaiah, a Jewish prophet, wrote, "This is what the Sovereign Lord, the Holy One of Israel, says: 'Only in returning to me and resting in me will you be saved. In quietness and confidence is your strength'" (Isaiah 30:15 NLT). And "Righteousness will bring peace. Yes, it will bring quietness and confidence forever" (Isaiah 32:17 NLT).

I see David and Isaiah each proclaim that "still waters" and "quietness" must be considered in crisis management. Thankfully, I do not have to provide the needed strength to endure; God has promised to hold me close and protect me. I marvel that He loves me and holds me securely, even though I may yell and scream my resistance or have a pouting attack. As I look back, I can affirm that He truly does provide peace and joy in every situation. But I must admit that I don't always look for or accept it.

David understands the seemingly innate stubbornness of human beings when he writes, "He makes me lie down in green pastures" (Psalm 23:2 NIV) That brings to mind another contradiction in my life. Why do I refuse the rest and the green pastures when those two ingredients are exactly what I need for rest and refreshment? Why do I insist on doing it my way —always the hard way?

Look at those exquisite hummingbirds! They aren't supposed to be able to fly. And their colors are drab until they turn, allowing the sun to reveal their iridescence. It would be phenomenal to see their nest and watch their babies. Now that is worth a spot on my bucket list.

In the process of accumulating lots of life experience, I have seen a wide variety of dark valleys. I know the valley of financial uncertainty with its scary, dark places. Questions swirl around, making it hard to focus and trust. Dread becomes an unwelcome intruder on any trip to the mailbox. Reminders of due dates stretch one's patience and overwhelm decisions to remain calm.

I don't remember those treks going through green pastures; the scenery in my memory remains pretty desolate! But God invites me to see the quiet waters and to let their stillness seep into my frantic emotions, calming me. What are some of the still waters He has shown me in that desert? Cash in an envelope with no name or return address. The realization that we never missed a mortgage payment. Gratitude for a bumper crop in our garden. An unexpected peace and assurance of God's faithfulness to His promises.

This afternoon has been delightful. It is time to head back. Back on the farm, we were privileged that our acreage included a beautiful woodsy area where we pastured the cows spring, summer, and fall. My family also spent happy times there—swimming, picnicking, exploring. My sister Lynn and I loved galloping on the Stagecoach Trail, our name for a narrow path that followed one of the ravines. Notice our path narrows here, skirting a small rockslide. Those sharp edges look dangerous. I am grateful we have a safe way around them.

You know, that rockslide reminds me of other valleys I have toured. Each rock and boulder could represent different sharp encounters. For example, the pain, regret, and remorse of unresolved rocky relationships readily bubbles to the surface. What still waters can be found in that valley? Humility, compassion, and empathy as I still must accept my failures and my inability to resolve problems.

And other rocks could be labeled—parenting challenges, failures, loneliness, times of waiting—and the list can go on. But let's focus on the delights of the day. Peace is a choice I choose to accept. And your companionship today has definitely refreshed me like green pastures and still waters. Thank you.

A Quiet Lake and Happy Little Clouds

Good morning. Ready for a leisurely ride? We can meander around this quiet lake in the little red paddleboat. Let's put the sun shade up here at the pier rather than trying to do that in the middle of the lake. Or a dip in the lake might provide refreshment—a little more excitement? What do you think? Are you up for an adventure?

I am surprised by the amount of talking I have done. Obviously, you are a very empathetic listener. Thank you for your kindness. I am not really comfortable talking about myself this much. But I need to share what I have learned in a dark valley I have visited way more often than I would ever choose—the dark valley of cancer.

You know part of Nancy's last trek through that valley, and you know I too shared a cancer diagnosis. I would rather not talk about cancer, but I urgently must share the hope encountered there—to share a journey that has included finding peace and joy in hidden green pastures and beside quiet waters as God walked through those valleys with me.

Let's drift into these reeds. I want to get a closer view of the red-winged blackbirds. They always kept me company when I was herding the cows in the alfalfa field back on the farm, and I have always considered them personal friends. They were easy to spot, and I could always identify their song.

Maybe we will see a yellow-headed blackbird today. I first saw one a long time ago at Bear Butte Lake in South Dakota. And I did see a pair here a few years back. They are fascinating and unexpected—kind of a mix between a giant canary and a crow.

Earlier accounts of my uterine cancer and Nancy's pancreatic cancer are really just the tip of our looming iceberg. Before either diagnosis, she and I experienced numerous storms of cancer invading our family. Both Mother and Father fought cancer. Mother had pancreatic cancer that was not officially confirmed until after her too-early death at age fifty-two. The medical profession knew so little about it. A few years later, Dad developed cancer of the pharynx and Non-Hodgkin's lymphoma. Even in that short time, great strides were being made in learning about and fighting cancer, but Dad died at age fifty-eight, five years after Mother. Watching anyone fight and lose to cancer is always traumatic, confusing, and painful, but especially a parent whose job has always been to protect you. We knew so little.

As if Mother and Dad's youth wasn't enough to demonstrate the dastardly impact of cancer, our older brother, Dan, at age forty-nine, had colon cancer—successfully fighting through surgery and chemotherapy. Around that same time, our younger sister Lynn, then only thirty-eight, was diagnosed with advanced ovarian cancer. She was not able to successfully fight that diagnosis. In less than four months, she left behind her husband and their two preschool children.

It is so tranquil out here in nature. Look at those pine siskins' ability to balance on such slender cattail reeds. Their bobbing is like a metronome for the soothing symphony being created. A bullfrog is positioning his bass drum while the frog chorus rehearses the opening song.

Three Truths Deeply Imprinted

Watching my mother's fight with cancer was the most traumatic experience in my first two and a half decades on earth. It was surreal and shook me to my core. It took years for the shock to wear off so that I could even begin to process my grief.

But in that traumatic valley, God surprised me with insight and growth in the green pastures and beside the still waters. There I began my personal journey toward wholeness. The earthquake of loss cracked a shell I had plastered around myself—a shell designed to protect me from pain and to keep me safe. But that shell kept me from authentic living. My clam would never again be completely watertight. That's when light began to leak into my shell. I had to admit that to be truly alive is about love, and love requires being open to risk. The truth? *Love demands risk.* Risk is scary, but God clearly promises His presence, love, and ultimate protection.

Another truth beside still waters? *Anger is not a sin.* I can and must be honest about my anger, especially my anger toward God. "Why did you allow the cancer? Why didn't You heal her? Why aren't You listening to me? I can't bear watching my father's pain." My volcanic emotions spewed anger. I really told God what I thought.

And you know what? While I raged, God enfolded me in His loving arms and said, "I know. This is painful for you. It is painful for Me too." He did not send me into time-out with a stern warning, "Stay there until you can be pleasant again." Instead, He held me until the pain and sobs lessened. He brought comfort in simple yet astonishing, ways. He helped me accept my emotions. And He encouraged, "Now, what shall we do with this pain?"

Shocked Midsentence

Having parented teens, I am still not sure whose job it is to embarrass whom. I know that parents don't have to try hard to embarrass young adolescent offspring. I clearly recall, as a young teen, being flabbergasted that my mother was forty. How could anyone be that old?

But twenty-seven years later when I turned forty, my incredulity wasn't about being old; it was that my next-younger sister could die. Incomprehensible! Now who would make clothes shopping a fun outing? Who would scour garage sales with me? Who would lead my cheer squad now? I needed her. Her husband and children needed her. The world needed her kindness, her beautiful voice, her enthusiasm, her joy.

And you can be sure that I pounded heaven's gates with one loud question. "God, why didn't You heal Lynn? I asked You to!"

I stopped to take a breath before continuing the interrogation. In that pause, I clearly heard God quietly say, "I did." And I had to simply shut my mouth. He did heal her. She was free of cancer and pain. My only conscious thought was, *Oh.* The lesson? *God answered my prayer.* He just didn't do it my way.

You may be wondering how often I hear voices in my head. How did I know it was God speaking? Because, obviously, the thought that stopped me midsentence did not logically come from my own brain. Ranting about my pain felt good, and I was on a roll. In that two-word reply, God stopped me with truth—a truth that shocked me as though I had plopped into a shallow pool of cold water. I sat in those still waters, knowing I couldn't deny the truth.

Goodness, the sun is high overhead. We need to head back so you can be on time to your appointment. Thank you for joining me on this lovely day. Thank you for being interested in my story.

A Delightful Visit to Grandmother and Grandfather

Good morning. Welcome to my grandparents' home. I unashamedly admit that my nostalgia makes it a little shrine-like. Everyone should be blessed with such precious, personal memories. I know that you shared an unbreakable bond with your own grandmother. You have spoken often about how safe and special you felt with her.

I loved visiting my grandparents. They lived in a small farming town in central Indiana about an hour from our home. Being in town was so different from our dairy farm in the country. At the time I was visiting them, farms were not illuminated with dusk-to-dawn LED lights. The streetlights at Grandma and Grandpa's house were so friendly. Every night, they peeked in to make sure we were sleeping soundly.

There were sidewalks, and we could walk to the post office. We felt really grown-up when Grandpa would trust us to go and get the mail. Peeking at the letters through the glass door, we felt so accomplished when we could make the combination work. Sometimes on our way back, we would walk past the ribbon factory and discover shiny bits of treasure!

Grandma's cookie jar always had huge, thick sugar cookies that she baked following the recipe found only in her head. I have tried to make those cookies but have never succeeded, even after watching her and taking notes several times. I can offer you a really good snickerdoodle.

After staying overnight, breakfast was amazing because I could have as many slices of toast as I wanted. With six children in our family, toast must have been rationed. Not at Grandma and Grandpa's home. Grandma's kitchen meant love and comfort.

I have been blessed with that comfort blanket as a foundational building block in my life. Through my family, God firmly established my understanding of His comfort. I have drawn on that comfort throughout my entire life.

I drew on that comfort in January 1995 when at age forty-eight the doctor said, "You have uterine cancer." I drew on that comfort in 1996 at the age of forty-nine when the doctor said, "We must perform a lumpectomy to remove the cancer in your left breast." I drew on that comfort five years later when the doctor said, "We will remove your squamous skin cancer with Moh's surgery." Again in 2002, after I had turned fifty-five, I needed that comfort base to bolster me after the doctor gave me a photo of the cancer in my bladder. A fifth diagnosis came in 2014: "You have colon cancer." That bout ended up being much more than I bargained for—being in and out and back into the hospital for a large part of September. Still, God proved Himself faithful to His promises and provided peace and joy.

I figured that having a full hand count of cancer was plenty. But in 2016, I had another encounter with squamous cell skin cancer followed by cancer in my right breast. I guess all of this establishes the fact that I am intimately acquainted with cancer. It is a good thing that God doesn't allot only a limited quota of comfort for each of us.

Memories of love and fun at Grandma and Grandpa's house

Since I have taught *The Adventures of Tom Sawyer* more than fifty times, Mark Twain is now my friend. His remarks after a visit to his childhood home match my experience now as we sit on the porch of Grandma and Grandpa's house. He said, "Nothing remains the same. When a man goes back to look at the house of his childhood, it has always shrunk; there is no instance of such a house being as big as the picture in memory and imagination."

This house may not be the mansion I thought it was, but that doesn't make any difference. The porch is still here, and we can still enjoy the porch swing. Just don't let Grandma hear us swing too high.

Another indelibly beautiful memory from Grandma and Grandpa's house is the cooing of mourning doves. So beautiful and so sad. My current home—a cute, not too big, brown-brick house in a small town—has sidewalks and friendly streetlights. It also has the third must for a proper home—mourning doves that sing of comfort.

One of the hardest pathways in my cancer journey has been the shock, pain, and unpredictability of grief. I think grief is a bigger monster than cancer. Grief brings confusion and sadness; it leaves reality toppled on its head so you really don't know if you are coming or going. If I am in a tornado, I will not be surprised by its force, because I have already been entrapped by grief as it swirls furiously, then suddenly disappears. It is sinisterly unpredictable and leaves disastrous debris.

And cancer has continued to give me grief. In 2010, my youngest sister, and in 2015, my older brother each lost their battles with cancer. But God has continued to help me find the green meadows and quiet stream as He comforts me along the way with part of a song, an unexpected note from a friend, a reminder of His presence and help, a good book, turning a stranger into a friend. He brings treasure and beauty out of pain and sorrow by giving me special opportunities to walk alongside others on the pathway of grief. I am very thankful for that; it is humbling and priceless to have something to offer another person at a time when no words can be found. I am so glad that God doesn't waste pain.

What helps one deal with grief? The first help I received were other people who stood with me or walked along with me. Eventually, I was able to examine grief more objectively and dissect it into more manageable parts. It takes time.

What is grief? A definition that I return to time and time again is by Ira J. Tanner in his book *The Gift of Grief*. He says that "grief is an emotional reaction to change and all change creates loss." He spends quite a bit of time exploring the breadth of the grief experience. He reminds the reader that grief is an emotion—neither right nor wrong. It simply exists.

Our culture is very uncomfortable with grief and has very strict rules. We are granted a short time to grieve the death of a person, but then you should be over it. But grief is much more comprehensive than our culture allows. Tanner points out that grief is inherent in a move or the loss of a dream. It is found in any change to life's circumstances. In fact, achieving an Olympic gold medal can leave the athlete on the precipice of grief as they now must deal with the loss of a driving goal. When we broaden our understanding of grief, we can be much more compassionate and truly human.

A person never gets over their grief. Yes, time allows us to move forward with our lives, but grief forever changes me and changes me and changes me. Most of the time, I am becoming more at peace with that.

There is no set time to finish grieving. In fact, it was ten years after my mother's death before I really even began the grief work I needed to do. I had already come to acceptance of my father's death, and he had died five years after my mother. I feared I was losing my mind and was sure that anyone who knew what was going on inside of me would agree. But you cannot dictate when grief will rear its ugly head and demand attention!

Going through grief is nonnegotiable. There is no way around. Denial may work for years, but even then, grief must be trudged through. It truly is a journey through darkest valleys.

I am now grateful to have learned from grief. I have relied over and over again on God's promises to be with me. He has shown me pastures where I may feed and renew my energy. He has led me to waters that are quiet enough to drink from and be refreshed.

Listen. Do you hear that? Music is coming from the park down the street. Let's investigate. I wonder if a band is playing in the concert shell. Or it might be the ice-cream truck! I *love* butter pecan. What flavor do you feel like today?

It's even better than a band. It is happy children at play. How they love to run and play and climb and swing and balance. That is music to my eyes as well as my ears. I am glad we no longer must abide by the rule "Children must be seen and not heard." Let's sit in the gazebo for a bit. We won't disturb the children here.

Certifiably Weird

It is not unusual for people to wonder if I am from an alien planet. They shake their heads in dismay when I share that I love eighth graders. While it is a very hard age to be, it is also a time of dynamic growth and exciting changes. I love that eighth graders are "beginning to wake up." Their sense of humor, while definitely a work in progress, is refreshing and honest. They ask hard questions and offer insightful comments. But then their next question can leave you shaking your head in wonder and dismay, such as, "Are we doing anything today?" And you never know what they might say next. In sincere, good faith, a student offered help to one of my younger colleagues: "I can help you find a more stylish way to wear your hair." Gotta love 'em!

Another fact to reinforce my weirdness is that I get excited teaching grammar. Most people immediately establish grammar as a taboo topic of conversation when they avow, "English was my worst subject in school." But if you want to see my normally calm demeanor become animated, just ask about my newest plan to help students innately understand the difference between action verbs, linking verbs, and verbs of being. (Okay, I'll stop; you are safe.)

Now comes the final evidence to the list of my weird perspectives: I don't hate cancer.

Yes, you read that correctly. I don't hate cancer. How can I hate that which has fertilized growth, brought reality into sharper focus, opened my eyes to untold riches? How can I hate that which has shown me just how precious life and love are?

The dark valleys of cancer have indelibly influenced my understanding of life. I do not view cancer as a sour note creating disharmony. Instead, I hear the counterpoint it provides. Cancer brings surprise and change and depth to my life's song. Its contrast provides an opportunity to examine and realign my perspectives.

We have had another delightful visit. Your compassionate listening has provided safety for me to share memories of hard times. Thank you.

Why Is Life So Messy?

I'm glad we decided to stop by the coffee shop to chat today. I would rather chew my calories than drink them, so I'll have the house special blend—black. In fact, I have saved up enough calories this week to order a cookie today. Oh, yes!

Time to talk about poetry again. I greatly enjoy the works of Robert Frost, Jack Prelutsky, Dr. Seuss, and, of course, Shel Silverstein. I find their messages easy to understand, and I can relate to their poetry. Poets express ideas and feelings common to humans through the use of carefully chosen words that they then arrange, making the most of sound, rhythm, and meaning. They highlight experiences and emotions that pull us together, thereby strengthening our connections. As I think about what a poem is saying to me, I also wonder what your thoughts might be. And I wonder, *How does your experience broaden mine?*

Shel Silverstein, known for whimsey in his writing, wrote a poem about Sarah Cynthia Sylvia Stout that emphasizes there are distasteful parts to life. This poem highlights the plight of a young girl who would willingly work hard in the kitchen but hated to take the garbage out. The consequences of the eventual mountain of garbage were very sad.

> And finally, Sarah Cynthia Stout said,
> "OK, I'll take the garbage out!"
> But then of course, it was too late …
> The garbage reached across the state,
> And there, in the garbage she did hate,
> Poor Sarah met an awful fate
> That I cannot right now relate
> Because the hour is much too late.

Life can seem so topsy-turvy. Children long to be grown-up—a time of freedom—when a person will finally be able to live life on his terms, be her own boss. Adults look back to childhood and long for the freedom from bills and work and decisions and responsibilities. Just like Sarah Cynthia Sylvia Stout, adults learn that there is a lot of messiness in the process of living life. At times, the route is straight, smooth, and simple. But congestion, construction, and convolutions always come, digging up so many questions. What happened? What went wrong? Where is the pathway?

Struggling and striving are a normal part of forward movement. Storms and rain come before a rainbow. Bread must be kneaded to activate the yeast. Digging a hole in the ground comes before the house foundation is poured. Eggs must be beaten before the soufflé can rise. Glass must be tempered before it becomes a windshield. Iron ore faces incredibly high temperatures on its way to becoming steel. A caterpillar must undergo a compete transformation in order to experience life as a butterfly.

Oh, good, here comes Rosa. I hoped she could join us. I have been so blessed with amazing friends. And I enjoy sharing these special people with anyone else who needs a friend. She and I began our friendship by throwing lifelines to each other when our children were young, when we felt so overwhelmed and helpless.

Conversation is sure to be stimulating with Rosa here. An extrovert, she is genuinely interested in every person she meets and has a gift for putting each in the center of her attention. If conversation lulls after catching up on the details of your week, Rosa always has at least two or three questions tucked into her pocket to pump energy back into the discussion. "What are you reading now? Do you untie your sneakers before you take them off or before you put them on? What energizes you? What makes you feel cared for?"

Rosa was the first to challenge me to learn to love the questions in life. She introduced me to the writing of Rainer Maria Rilke, who wrote this:

> Be patient toward all that is unsolved in your heart and try to love the questions themselves ... Do not now seek the answers, which cannot be given you because you would not be able to live them ... Live the questions now. Perhaps you will then gradually, without noticing it, live along some distant day into the answer.

Eventually, I have become much more comfortable with questions, even those without an answer.

Rosa has thrown out some challenging questions today. What is peace? What does joy look like in real life? Can peace and joy exist in chaos?

I must warn you; I am much better at asking the questions than giving a satisfying answer. I will not pretend to have definitive answers in five words or less. But I love a good discussion, a thoughtful interchange of ideas, a challenge of perspective. Shall we dive in?

Challenge number one: what is peace? Just as children wistfully dream of having adult freedoms, adults often depict peace as a person sitting on a quiet beach that is being gently tickled by the ocean while watching the interplay of brilliant and muted sunset colors. But peace and protection can be found in the midst of a furious storm.

The picture painted by Jack E. Dawson in 1996 called *Peace in the Midst of the Storm* provides challenging food for thought. It depicts a furious storm with lightning, thunder, and water hurling over high rocks, crashing below. In the midst of that chaos, a bird sits calmly on her nest in an almost hidden niche, serenely protecting her chicks. This picture challenges the often held idea that peace must include the absence of turmoil and danger.

But what is peace? True peace is a surety within my inner self that is not shaken by adversity, befogged by regrets, or disturbed by fear. Jesus Christ promised sure and deep peace. "Peace I leave with you; my peace I give you. I do not give to you as the world gives. Do not let your hearts be troubled and do not be afraid" (John 14:27 NIV). And the apostle Paul tells us that the peace of God goes beyond our ability to understand. "Rejoice in the Lord always. I will say it again: Rejoice! Let your gentleness be evident to all. The Lord is near. Do not be anxious about anything, but in every situation, by prayer and petition, with thanksgiving, present your requests to God. And the peace of God, which transcends all understanding, will guard your hearts and your minds in Christ Jesus" (Philippians 4:4–7 NIV). Where God is, there is peace.

Challenge number two: what is joy? Understanding joy is complex for me. I stayed away from this writing for several weeks as I struggled to craft my definition. I finally decided to be honest with myself and admit that I cannot clearly explain joy for all the world to understand. But I can share my experiences. I have seen and experienced joy.

True joy is not an emotion coming from a sense of well-being, success, or good fortune or from expecting good things to happen. It is much more. Joy allows me to experience life as a marvelous adventure and see the world as a friendly home. Today, I saw pure joy radiating from our three-year-old grandson as he ran and jumped into a pile of leaves that he had helped rake. And remember the deep belly laughs of babies? They are joy. I feel the joy of hope each year when spring returns. Birds sing for joy, and pansies' faces beam joy and beauty. True joy—in so many places.

But I struggle with two contrasting ideas about joy. First, I have a responsibility to joy—I must choose joy. Searching the book of Psalms to examine what David said about joy, I recorded more than sixty verses. He wrote, "Shout for joy to God, all the earth!" (Psalm 66:1 NIV) and, "My lips will shout for joy when I sing praise to you" (Psalm 71:23 NIV). And the apostle Paul echoes, "Rejoice in the Lord always. I will say it again; Rejoice" (Philippians 4:4 NIV). Those are instructions and commands, not just suggestions. It is clear that I have a responsibility in the joy process.

To encourage means to "put courage into." Encouraging a friend includes reminding her of times she found and used courage. And then you specifically remind her of the courage she has now. Rejoicing with that friend means to "rehearse times of joy" together. It involves remembering joys and thus experiencing those joys again. You "re-joy" together.

The luncheon after Nancy's funeral remains one of my most poignant memories. The service was in a rural Indiana church with salt of the earth people who were *amazing* cooks. The lunch was a truly old-fashioned potluck. Going into the fellowship hall, we were greeted by a buffet line that was at least four big tables long. Every available space was filled with fragrant gifts, each different from the other. There wasn't even room for decorations. The food provided plenty of eye candy.

And that array of food didn't include the beverages or the desserts. Oh, my! We feasted on food and memories and being together. Here is a conversation between myself and my heavenly Father.

"Choose the table"

Her Concern:
>Father, I am too tired to even look up or ask for help. Life right now is siphoning all energy. Even my reserve tanks are vapors. I want to follow Your instructions and complete the tasks You have given me. I value the tasks and consider each an honor to have, but I am weak and helpless.

Her Father's Reply:
>The tasks I give are not burdensome.

Her Question:
>But what does that mean? What of hard, physical work? Difficult mental work? Draining emotional work? Are not those heavy? I do not understand.

Her Father's Reply:
>It is always My plan for lessons and tasks to come in the easiest form possible. When you will go your own way and push aside my counsel, the lesson or task seems more rigid. It is your pushing that increases the restraint—revealing the barriers.

Her Memory:
>The loss of my loved ones are times that stand out. I remember each of those times as being truly hard. There was no way around them. And I know they were not sent as a lesson to learn, a test to pass, or a reprimand for sin. They were an inevitable fact of life. I think I have learned that Your plan for those times includes acknowledging the situation, accepting it rather than denying it, and trusting You for understanding and comfort. And You have always helped me and walked with me. You have always been faithful to make Your love felt.

Her Father's Reply:
>Thank you, My daughter, for remembering My love. What else do you remember?

Her Memory:
>I remember the enormous table of food (community love) at Nancy's memorial celebration. With David, I can say, "You prepare a table for me in the midst of my enemies (or hard times)."

Her Father's Reply:
>And why have I brought that powerful picture to your mind?

Her Answer:
>You want me to remember that I have a choice. I can focus on the table or on the difficult task.

Her Plea:
>Father, help me to choose the table.

In contrast to the command to find joy, I see that joy is also a gift, one that comes unbidden, a surprise. I cannot dictate its arrival. My very act of trying to create joy causes it to evaporate. C. S. Lewis insists, "Joy is distinct not only from pleasure in general but even from aesthetic pleasure. It must have the stab, the pang, the inconsolable longing." Joy is a gift from God and a fruit of His Spirit.

My most recent encounter with cancer surprised me by dragging along a sense of dread; I didn't want to go through "this" again. My head accepted the situation, grateful for a highly skilled medical team. I was confident in my surgeon, in awe of my oncologist, and thankful for a very supportive family. But my heart and my emotions seemed able to only shuffle their feet in reluctance. My usual optimism hid in a closet somewhere and refused to be found so I could begin to coax it out. I had lost my joy.

Thankfully, I have not been plagued by the "Why me?" question. I have not seen cancer as a punishment. I have not been singled out with an unfair problem. I figure that since the sun shines on the just and the unjust, it is logical that storms beset the just and the unjust as well. Why should I escape the problems of life? Everyone has challenges. Besides, who are the just?

But this time, cancer's pathway loomed with a specter that I couldn't seem to banish. Most of my friends will affirm that I am a positive-attitude person. I innately love the challenge of finding a genuinely productive way to look at any situation. This time, my search was fruitless *until* ...

Have you ever noticed how at times a theme or an idea keeps popping up in seemingly random and unrelated places? For at least a week, it seemed that everything I read, heard, or people I talked to somehow pointed to the theme of finding my pathway. Conversations with random friends and acquaintances cycled around to gaining direction regarding life or a challenge or a decision. Widely diverse print sources and unexpected programs seemed to have the same theme, designed just for me.

One day, I even "heard" my dad's voice saying, "This is the way; walk in it." That memory caused me to wonder if Dad was quoting from the Bible or if it was his personal interpretation. So I went searching. I was not surprised to find it in the book of Isaiah. "Whether you turn to the right or to the left, your ears will hear a voice behind you saying, 'This is the way; walk in it'" (Isaiah 30:21 NIV).

All of these messages were swirling around me as I sat in church the day before I was to begin radiation. I don't remember whether we were singing or the pastor was giving his sermon or what was happening around me. But all at once, everything clearly came together. The path ahead of me was the best one for me to follow because God knew about it and was going with me. That path led through green meadows and along quiet streams in a very dark valley. But the valley could only cast a shadow; it couldn't stop my forward movement. Suddenly, I was eager to go that way.

At that point, joy erupted and bubbled over! That return was completely unexpected; it was not something I could have made happen on my own. When I agreed that God's way is very good and affirmed that I chose to follow His way, God sent joy to illuminate that hard pathway.

Can peace and joy exist in chaos? Yes, peace and joy do exist amid chaos! I treasure a peaceful summer evening on the patio, enjoying the gardens and evening sounds (obviously, with no mosquitoes). But I can assure you that peace and joy exist even in the midst of chaos. Where does that peace come from? I find it in the assurance of God's love for me, a love much deeper than I can fathom. The truth of His love inspires confidence. And because of that truth, I can be patient and wait to find answers to the many questions that bombard me.

The Cure

My story, in a nutshell, is a demonstration of two great weaknesses. I share a chromosomal weakness with many family members; it's named Lynch syndrome. This genetic marker indicates a high risk of developing cancer of the colorectal family and perhaps other types of cancer. The Lynch gene does not guarantee getting cancer; it is just a marker. It signals that being vigilant and proactive are imperative. The positive side is that survival rates are very high for individuals who know they carry this marker. My medical team and I maintain vigilance with a consistent monitoring schedule.

Heredity dealt me a bad gene, but must I be resigned to it? Must I give it power? No. I choose to trust God. Even for the hard places in life, I surrender outcomes to God's plan. Am I strange? Perhaps, but I am not alone. Jesus Christ chose the hard path of obedience to achieve God's final goal. "For the joy set before Him he endured the cross, scorning its shame, and sat down at the right hand of the throne of God" (Hebrews 12:2 NIV).

My second weakness? My humanity. I don't do what I know is good, and I easily do those things that are wrong and harmful. I love chocolate; I hate dieting. I don't want to exercise; relaxing is more fun. I feel anger toward people who love me most, those who want the best for me. Why am I that way? Why am I so weak? How do I fight that weakness?

The cure is God's perfect love. But how can perfection associate with weakness and human frailty? Doesn't the fact that He loves me imply He isn't perfect? Doesn't that very desire for association taint His perfection?

Surprisingly, God agrees that I have a valid question. I cannot look directly into the sun; I must use a shield to protect my eyes. In that same way, God cannot look on sin. That's where Jesus Christ changes the picture. Because I have agreed that I need help and have trusted Christ as my advocate, God can now look at me because my sins are shielded (covered) by Christ's sacrifice.

Now I have complete access to God; He can see me. I can survive, thrive, and conquer because God gives strength where I am weak. And I can rely on the certainty of that strength because He gives freely and without reservation. I can trust His loving heart because "There is no fear in love ... perfect love drives out fear" (1 John 4:18a NIV).

Not Hate, Not Fear

In a sermon a few months ago about surviving hard times, the pastor pointed out that God's admonition (or his angel's) to "fear not" can be found 365 times in the Bible—one for each day of the year. And how to defeat fear? Take action. Go on the offensive by trusting. Jesus reminds me, "Do not let your hearts be troubled. You believe in God; believe also in me" (John 14:1 NIV).

I do not hate cancer, and I choose not to live in fear of cancer. I choose to be thankful for life.

Epilogue

April 30, 2003, we unwillingly said goodbye to Nancy. She died peacefully at home, surrounded by clouds of love. She didn't want to leave her loved ones but was ready to go. We didn't want her to leave but did want healing and peace for her. And we knew she was welcomed by a host of loved ones who had gone before.

Who's the Teacher?

Nancy continued to teach me about life. She showed me perseverance and then showed me how to die. It is apparent that Nancy's world never narrowed. We have listened to her faith in a holy and loving God, her love for His Son, Jesus Christ, and her appreciation for the guidance she received by His Holy Spirit. Her body became more confining, but her spirit soared, whether singing or listening to music, contemplating and finding encouragement in a message or book, giving a hug to someone who was sad or happy, and sharing what she was learning from God. While it was increasingly hard for her to get out, she actively continued to live—reading, calling a friend, praying for the many people she loved, listening to God, reading God's Word, and writing notes, cards, and letters.

Upon arriving in heaven, I am sure Nancy immediately saw God with His arms open wide and heard Him say, "Well done, good and faithful servant" (Matthew 25:21 NIV). There is no higher commendation.

Because I Forget So Easily

I know intimately that just a few seconds can change my life, so why do I forget and take it for granted? Why do I let my focus drift away from the essentials? *Every day*, I must intentionally remind myself to …

Give thanks for the present. And what does it look like to "be present in the present"? It includes taking time to be with each person I encounter—stopping to appreciate the delectable aroma of freshly baked chocolate chip cookies, savoring the safe-inside-and-protected feeling during a furious storm, intentionally noticing and appreciating each minute of life. In reality, that's all I have.

Let love reign in my life. I must not let fear stop me from loving. Perfect love casts out fear. Love is a gift that I must accept and open on a daily basis.

Choose joy continuously. That includes slowing down to enjoy the moment (put joy into, recall previous joy). Let patience and perseverance keep growing.

Be as kind to each person I meet, as much as possible. Be especially kind to the person in my mirror at home. Find rest. Do things that bring me refreshment. Make time for people and activities that nourish and rejuvenate me.